Make a Splash

Swimming holes and Waterfalls
of the
Green Mountains

Jason Minor

Disclaimer

Engaging in any activity around water has inherent risks. The publisher and author of this book in no way guarantees the safety of any route, trail, path, swimming area or natural area in this book. Since these areas are always changing, visitors must use their own judgments when determining and assessing the conditions and safety of any route, trail, path, swimming area or natural area.

Users of this book must not trespass on any natural area, should it become posted.

MS Master Studios

Cover photo: Megan Lovell and Jonathan Merrey relax in the warm summer sun at Bingham Falls in Stowe.

Invitation to readers:

I am committed to protecting the natural treasures in this book and can do so only with your help. If you should discover any changes that have occurred with these areas please let me know so that corrections can be made for future editions.

— Jason Minor

For additional copies, please write:

Jason Minor
RR1 Box 260
Swanton, VT 05488

Library of Congress Cataloging-in-Publication Data

Make a Splash: Swimming Holes and Waterfalls of the
    Green Mountains
    p. cm.
    Includes index
Minor, Jason 1971—
    LC 98-91299
    ISBN 0-9663556-0-1
    1. Travel & travel guides
    (pbk.)   98-4100

Book design by Jason Minor
Proofreaders: Bill Jacko, Marshall Matlock

Photographs, illustrations © Jason Minor

Printed in Canada
Published by Master Studios

Acknowledgements

A special thanks to the following people, for without them this book would not have been possible:

My mom for her encouragement and support, my brother for not asking me: Got a job yet? Gabby Varmette for the grab-the-bull-by-the-horns advice and for being a rock in a sea of Java, Stephanie Cunningham for her keen eye and mind, Marshall Matlock for pulling the thorns from my side, Karen Pardee for her unparalleled compassion, Kimi LaFleur for making me who I am, Kaybeth Stacey for never believing what she read about me in the paper, Jo Roback and Amy McVey for allowing me to polish my skills on their emery board, Hillard Land Jr. for opening his doors and mine in the process, Art and Joyce Seace for reminding me of what a great place Vermont is, Doug Wonders for his constant support and guidance, David Sutherland for the lack of faith that forced me to prove him wrong, Russ Phillips for making photography fun, Kevin Kelly for being the standard by which to determine insanity, Jon Wagner for his ears and advice, Bill Jacko for his eye for missing ink blotches, the Montgomery flood victims for defining the word determination, Jake Hubbard for his expertise, mother nature for all her wonderful gifts, and all of the landowners for their commitment to sharing nature's beauty. Thank you all. You have given me and everyone who reads this book something we can never repay — for that I am eternally grateful.

Table of Contents

preface:

northern region:

Table of Contents

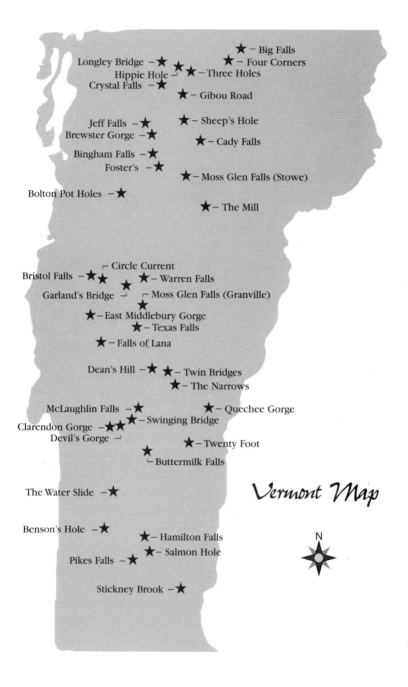

★ – Big Falls
Longley Bridge – ★   ★ – Four Corners
Hippie Hole – ★ ★ – Three Holes
Crystal Falls – ★
★ – Gibou Road

Jeff Falls – ★   ★ – Sheep's Hole
Brewster Gorge – ★
★ – Cady Falls
Bingham Falls – ★
Foster's – ★
★ – Moss Glen Falls (Stowe)
Bolton Pot Holes – ★
★ – The Mill

Circle Current
Bristol Falls – ★★   ★ – Warren Falls
Garland's Bridge – ★   ★ – Moss Glen Falls (Granville)
★
★ – East Middlebury Gorge
★ – Texas Falls
★ – Falls of Lana

Dean's Hill – ★ ★ – Twin Bridges
★ – The Narrows

McLaughlin Falls – ★   ★ – Quechee Gorge
Clarendon Gorge – ★★ ★ – Swinging Bridge
Devil's Gorge – ★
★ – Twenty Foot
★
★ Buttermilk Falls

The Water Slide – ★

Benson's Hole – ★
★ – Hamilton Falls
★ – Salmon Hole
Pikes Falls – ★
Stickney Brook – ★

Vermont Map

N

Katie Kenworthy slides down a waterfall in central Vermont. This is something you shouldn't try.

Michael Brailey examines his catch. Dace and brook trout filled his net more than once on this afternoon.

Introduction

If you follow water on its silvery, serpentine way down a mountain, you will discover chutes and gorges that thunder with the primordial roars of gods.

Occasionally, the headwaters will meander under the shade of maple trees and through the dark spruce forests, untouched by man's machines. As you wander so does the river, cutting left to right, following the path of least resistance through once forested fields of clover that meet the sky in the distance. Even farther on, you will be forced from the water's shore by steep chasms that allow only water and debris to pass through them safely.

To continue on your journey, you must leave the water's edge and walk around the gulch. Your anticipation beckons your imagination as to what you will discover at the base of the rushing water. The ground beneath you shakes, and you hear the sound of rushing water — not with just your ears but with your body.

From the top of the rise, you see an emerald pool surrounded by moisture-hungry trees. The tranquil nature of the pool is in direct conflict with what you hear and feel. The embankment is steep and treacherous, but you carefully reach the shore. You take your eyes off your feet and shrink in the presence of a twenty-foot waterfall.

The water near you is cool, calm and inviting; tired and hot, you jump in. The sweat from your body mingles with the water on its continuing journey. But for now you enjoy the water's cold caress.

I will come here often, you think, because I feel alive and a part of nature. Looking up at the twenty-foot waterfall, you feel small and powerless — perhaps how our ancestors felt in the company of a vast and unexplored wilderness. There is a connection with people here you can't explain. You have never felt more aware of your being. The fresh chill of the water numbs your nerves.

As you continue on your journey, all you can think about is sharing your discovery with a friend and about finding more places like this.

★ ★ ★

After a long hard winter in the North Country, nothing

signals the change of season more eloquently than the spring runoffs.

Waterfalls and swimming holes are reborn with the jubilation of rambunctious puppies. Swimming holes are the heart and soul of youth and vitality. They start anew each year when they give birth to the spring waters that carry the nutrients that make life possible.

I want to share with you my favorite spots. And in doing so, I hope you will develop an appreciation for these natural areas and help to protect them in the future.

I have included chapters on etiquette and safety to ensure that these areas remain accessible. Remember, most of these areas are accessible only because landowners have allowed them to be. This understanding is crucial to the long-term stability of swimming holes.

Each area in this book has a unique and cherished history. If we work together, we can ensure that our children can be a part of history at these areas as well.

Books and sandals go hand in hand with relaxing and sun bathing at Bristol Falls.

How to use this book

To help with trip planning, I have included guides to help you select swimming holes to visit, and then how to find the spot you have picked to visit. While I have included a lot of information and have rated each location, this information is just a starting point and doesn't take the place of sound judgment and common sense. For example, don't use my description of pool size and depth as a gauge to determine where to jump. Pool size and depth is merely one category that helps you decide if you want to visit a swimming hole or whether you can swim at a hole.

Directions

You can approach many of these swimming holes from several directions, so I have picked the most common route, normally from the nearest town.

Parking

I have listed places to park for each site. Parking areas, like swimming holes, can change seasonally. A site with room for five cars in early June may be full in mid-July. If a swimming hole is crowded beyond the carrying capacity of the parking area, then go to the next closest swimming hole. It is important to use good judgment and always obey parking signs. *Our parking behavior at swimming holes is key to our continued access.* All it takes is one car parked on someone's lawn to ruin a swimming hole for everyone.

Locator guide

The *Vermont Atlas & Gazetteer* (Delorme, Freeport, ME) is an excellent guide to the back roads of Vermont. For that reason, I use it as a locator guide. For each site, I list three figures in parentheses that consist of the page number, grid number and special quadrant number for quick access. (Make sure that you have a current atlas to utilize the locator.)

For example, (Pg 52, D5, Q2) is for Longley Bridge in

Montgomery. To find the swimming hole, turn to page 52 (in the atlas); then, find where the D and 5 column meet to form the D5 grid; and finally, use the quadrant guide to find where the swimming hole is on the grid. (The quadrant is simply broken into four equal quarters. The top left is Q1. The top right is Q2. The bottom left is Q3. And the bottom right is Q4.)

Swimming area

Each listed swimming hole has a recommended swimming area. Since the power of the current, depth of the pools and amount of water in the pool is in a constant state of flux, remember to always investigate the pools before ever entering the water. This guide is intended only to help plan visits. It is not designed to be used by risk takers to determine safe depths for jumping. *As a general rule, never swim above a waterfall; and remember, all swimming holes are rated during normal summer flow.*

Visitor guide

I have used several categories to rate each site. Using a rating system (1 to 5 with 5 being the best), I scored the pool size and depth, the waterfalls, access and any unique features.

Size and depth of pool: The size of the pool relates to the overall surface area of water for either swimming or wading. At swimming holes with more than one pool, the sizes of the pools are totaled. For instance, a pool that is 50 square feet is equivalent to two 25-square-foot pools.

The other part of this category, depth, deals with whether swimming is possible. *Deep pools in this book are considered four feet and over.* Remember that this category provides a rough guide to two variables. For example, Cady falls is relatively large but shallow in most places. The size of the pool is so large that it scores a 5. A pool, then, can score high in this category yet still be very shallow. *Never use this category as a jumping guide!*

Number and height of waterfalls: This category also takes into consideration two factors in rating. A natural area in this book, for instance, can score high if it has only one tall waterfall. I rate Moss Glen Falls a 5 in this category because of the huge single waterfall. The Stickney Brook swimming hole is rated a 5 because of the sheer number of waterfalls.

Ease of location and access: The ease of location means both how easily a natural area is to find on a roadway and where it exists geographically. The natural areas that exist far from main or parking areas score lower in this category.

Access deals with two issues. One is whether the land is public or private; the other, is how easy it is to reach the water after parking. Several factors complicate the first issue. The first of which is whether the community knows the land as being open to the public. For instance, swimming holes on private land are still considered publicly accessible in this rating system if the landowner allows visitors to swim. Unless landowners make solid stands against visitors by posting their land, swimming holes known as open to the community are accessible the public. ***Just because a swimming hole is in this book, it doesn't necessarily mean that it will always be accessible.*** In case of doubt, ask permission first — ***never trespass. And always obey all landowners' requests on signs — (for examples see page 22).***

Uniqueness of features: This category examines historic and geologic features. I rate both features together based on how the surrounding area has been shaped by it, rather than how it occurs in nature. For instance, gorges are relatively common along mountain streams, but gorges that have carved potholes are not. That is why Bolton Potholes received a 5 in this category.

This category is very subjective. We might summarize it like this: Here's an interesting place to visit whether you swim or not.

It takes a minimum combined score of 10 for a swimming hole or waterfall to make it into this guidebook. Most of the sites score far above that. Unfortunately, I have excluded several popular swimming holes because of parking and access issues.

Calvin Carlisle takes a break from exploring the bottom of the New Haven river to laugh with his parents.

Safety

We seldom associate our leisure with danger. Yet in order to prevent injuries in and around swimming holes, it is important to be aware of certain activities that put visitors and swimmers at risk.

This chapter is neither a first aid manual nor an attempt to cover all of the dangers that present themselves around swimming holes. Instead, it's an awareness guide that will give swimmers some basic information in order to make sound judgments.

Water temperature is an often overlooked aspect of swimming holes. Since water temperatures in mountain streams rarely exceed 65-degrees Fahrenheit, swimmers should be aware of the possibility of hypothermia. Hypothermia at swimming holes is a result of physical contact between water and body, which results in loss of heat through conduction. It is very difficult to predict the rate at which conduction will cause hypothermia, because it depends on body size, water temperature and insulation factors. The risk to children, whose body temperatures are not as easily maintained because of their smaller size, is greater. So if you bring children to a mountain stream, monitor and limit the amount of time they spent in the water.

The most common minor injuries around swimming holes are caused from slips and falls on the rocks. A rock does not have to be wet to be slippery. In fact, most rocks are covered with algae or moss that make them naturally slick. These plant species thrive in the moist air that accompanies the waterfalls.

Keep in mind the water formed these areas and as a result, most rocks have been smoothed and polished providing little grip for even the best-soled pair of rock hoppers.

Lichen and algae make the rocks under the water extremely hazardous. It is nearly impossible to walk across a stream without slipping on a rock in one form or another. The safest way to traverse a waterway is to step on immovable objects that are flat and offer small convolutions to keep your foot from sliding. Watch where you step and avoid unnecessary scrapes and bruises.

When walking to the water, don't always assume the most

traveled path is the safest. It probably is the quickest. Trust your own judgment. In slick areas, always try to have at least two points of your body touching something solid at one time. If you must lift one foot to step on a lower rock, grab a solid tree or lean over and place a hand on the ground.

The most deceiving force at a swimming hole is the water itself. Water crashing into a pool doesn't necessarily sound dangerous — it can sound alluring or even romantic.

A problem arises when someone fails to respect the power of the current. To swimmers who have been carried by water against their will, there is nothing more frightening and dangerous. *Never swim above a waterfall.* This book rarely references a pool above a waterfall because it is usually unsafe.

Year after year, someone is swept over a waterfall after jumping into a pool above one. Try to avoid all upper and middle pools at swimming holes.

Never let a child near any waterfall or hidden pools unless accompanied by an adult. Watch children carefully. Only bring them to smaller swimming holes with safe pools.

Jumping or diving from rocks and trees kills and injures more people than any other activity at these natural areas. This dangerous activity has not only hurt the reputation of many areas, but it has also forced the closing of others. *Jumping is strongly discouraged.*

It is a long way to the emergency room from most of these spots. Remember to use your head and keep safety in mind as you enjoy these beautiful places to swim.

Amanda Breese, bottom, and Aimee MacMahon share a quiet afternoon on the rocks at Bristol Falls.

Parking at Bolton Potholes and other swimming holes around the state has created dangerous bottlenecks that have put access in jeopardy.

Etiquette

W hen the sun is right, the trail leading to the swimming hole at Brewster Gorge in Jeffersonville sparkles like the underside of minnows. It is not quartz particles causing the glare — it is broken beer and soda bottles. Why do people break glass on the very trail that carries them to the gorge? These acts have closed more than one Vermont swimming hole and threaten the access of many more. It is only a few who litter, but their lack of consideration impacts us all.

Most of the swimming holes listed in this book have been open to the public for decades. Until now, the only written rules of etiquette at swimming holes were printed on signs posted by landowners. As the popularity of these places grows, the importance of proper behavior becomes more important. Each careless toss of a soda can or violent heave of a glass bottle increases the likelihood that landowners will post their land, forbidding even the considerate locals from the area.

The most reasonable principle to follow is to act like we are guests in a friend's yard, and let our actions follow. After all, are we not guests at these areas? Are the landowners not our friends for letting us enjoy the wonders that they control?

It is in visitors' best interest to pick up a stray wrapper. A small concerted effort by many is better than an enormous effort by landowners. It doesn't take more than a few seasons for landowners to ask themselves, "Why should we bother picking up trash when we don't have to? We'll post it." With this in mind, try to leave a swimming hole cleaner than you found it.

Here is a simple code of conduct for swimming holes:

— I will use good driving manners getting to the site — keeping the speed and dust down on dirt roads.
— I will park only where there is off-road room for my vehicle. (Law in Vermont states that all wheels of a vehicle must be off the traveled portion of the road. If any part of the car remains on the road, it will either be towed or ticketed. Recently, the enforcement of parking near popular swimming

holes has limited visitors.)

— I will not litter. I will carry out what I carry in, and carry out more than my share when possible.

— I will avoid alcoholic beverages at swimming holes.

— I will not participate in or encourage cliff jumping or other dangerous stunts. If I see someone taking a risk, I'll ask them politely to stop.

— I will respect the privacy of other visitors.

— I will not participate in any activity that damages the natural area.

— I will not trespass on any posted property.

— I will obey all requests made by landowner and posted on signs.

Swimming hole etiquette comes down to this: Use common sense, show some respect and consideration for others and the land, and leave the place better than you found it.

Water flows through some of the most elegant falls in Vermont on its way down Mendon Peak.

A person temporarily leaves a mark on the landscape — much the same as rivers and streams do on the landscape.

Northern Region

For a moment a swimmer leaves a harmless mark on the land. A footprint on the surface of a polished rock slowly evaporates as the last towel is collected just before dark. The loud crash of the waterfall has turned to a dull, distant, and nearly unnoticeable roar by the time a slamming door signals the last goodbye.

The swimming hole stands resolute and strong under a cloudless sky. The night is a time of peace and contemplation.

So many have swam in the hole's cool pools and rested on its rugged shores. For now it seems, it has experienced every emotion.

It remembers when Suzy Baker nearly broke her leg after jumping off its north cliff; it remembers when Allen Reynolds screamed all the way over its waterfall; most of all it remembers, and holds most precious, when swimmers break the silence with euphoric laughter.

It feels a connection with the people and animals that come to its shores. The commonness that binds and unites the hole with visitors is mortality. Soon the yearly floods will change the path of the stream, taking away the water that has shaped it and given it life. That day may seem so very far away. But it will come. The first hemlocks that lined its shores began so boldly fighting for a few inches of sunlight. They all fell within its life span.

To many visitors, the swimming hole is alone and only alive when they are near. Much of that is true. It lives to socialize, to experience life before it is too late.

This quiet night is no different. Hours after the sun fell behind the western hill, a few giggles catch an owl's probing eye.

Two young lovers sit talking quietly, listening to the falls. The sound of their voices mingles in quiet competition with the falls. This is a night to remember. Suzy and Allen are no longer children. They sit on the rugged shores ready to leap into the world of adulthood — together.

In what seems like a mountain breeze, the swimming hole's melancholic sigh brushes the owl's feathers, raises goose bumps on the lovers' necks and carries away the last drop of water from the footprint .

Shawn Reynolds casts into the wind in an attempt to catch a brook trout. This evening he was unsuccessful.

Longley Bridge

Built in 1863, Longley Bridge crosses the Trout River. At approximately 89-feet long, it is Montgomery's longest covered bridge. The pool is located just below the bridge on the north side. Large rocks in the water serve as breakwater for the trout, and, as a result, it is a popular fly fishing spot.

The underside of the lattice-type bridge, a must see during any visit, illustrates the difference between a craftsman's workmanship and an engineer's. Everything has been hand pegged and cut.

The northeast side of the main pool on the sloping rock offers an excellent spot to relax. Sunbathers and fisherman frequent the rock, which offers sunlight for most of the afternoon.

On the south side of the main hole, cows drink from from the stream bank near the pasture. You get a real sense for what life was like long ago. The bridge, the livestock, the undeveloped river all point to an era free of traffic jams and skyscrapers.

Longley Bridge along with Comstock and Fuller were damaged during a flood in 1997. Incredibly, they remained standing even after the steel bridge in the center of the town collapsed. Ironically, the temporary bridge once constructed near the steel bridge uses the same principles of lattice support that covered bridges employ.

Directions: Longley Bridge is approximately 1 mile south of Montgomery Village. A trail leads east to the main swimming area
Parking: Available on the east side of the bridge as you pull off Route 118. (Pg 52, D5, Q2)
Swimming area: The main swimming area is below Longley Bridge, but some swimmers sunbathe on the northeast rock.

Visitor Guide:

Size & depth of pool: 4
No. & height of waterfalls: 1
Ease of location & access: 5
Uniqueness of features: 2

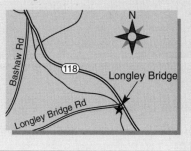

Ryan Burns flips into the Hippie Hole as friends Brendan O'Shea and Woody Wright-Moore, right, look on.

Hippie Hole

With perhaps one of the most interesting names in the state, Hippie Hole is a cherished local treasure. Whether the name came from the generation of free-spirited youngsters of the sixties is unknown. Little has changed here in the past thirty years, other than the swimsuits worn by visitors.

The crown jewel of the hole was once a balancing rock that rested beneath the hemlocks on a protuberance carved by the water, but the flood of 1997 moved the rock from its perch.

The waterway to the falls is about 35-feet long. When the water is low and the current weak, swimmers can swim part of the way to the falls. Several large boulders are wedged in the channel to prevent swimmers from reaching the falls. The water, which can rise over two feet after a light rain, has carved concave rock along the narrow waterway forming a mini-chasm.

Two main falls constitute a drop of about ten feet within a very short distance. The four-foot upper falls is quickly followed by the six-foot main falls adjacent to the pool.

(If there is more than one car at this swimming hole, visit on another day.)

Directions: Take Route 118 west about .4 of a mile from Montgomery Village. You will pass over a steel bridge. Take the next left onto West Hill Road, just before a second steel bridge. Go up the hill on the dirt road .2 of a mile. Follow the path over the west bank and to the left. (Pg 52, D5, Q4)

Parking: There is room for only three vehicles on the right side of the road only.

Swimming area: The main pool at the end of the channel leading to the falls offers the best swimming.

Visitor Guide:
Size & depth of pool: 3
No. & height of falls: 3
Ease of location & access: 3
Uniqueness of features: 3

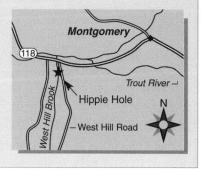

Elizabeth Davidson enjoys the natural bubble bath below Creamery Bridge at Crystal Falls in Montgomery.

Crystal Falls

Creamery Bridge is said to be haunted. Stepping onto this bridge is like traveling to a time when lovers sneaked out of their parents' homes to meet here and carve their initials in the trusses. Their moments in time are still visible. If the lovers are still here, maybe it's because this is where they found true love. Or maybe this is a place of peace.

One thing is for sure: If you stop and listen in the middle of the bridge, allowing the wooden trusses to stretch over your back, like the arms of all those lovers, you will soon lose sight of your problems.

Thoreau knew the importance of simplicity. At Creamery bridge, it is a treasure that seems within anyone's grasp.

The path to the water goes over the Jewett brothers' saw mill foundation. Over a hundred years ago, the brothers used water from the falls to power their mill to build the bridges around Montgomery.

The main pool is between a steep bank to the south and the foundation to the north. The pool and the 12-foot falls are extremely clear, perhaps giving birth to the name Crystal Falls. The water running over the falls shoots into the air near the water, offering a nice cool spray. As you look at the falls, the water pours over the sloping rock on the right side. Some swimmers slide from a shallow pool six feet into the main pool.

Directions: Take West Hill Road, between the second and the third steel bridge, 2.6 miles until you reach a four corners. Take a left onto Creamery Bridge Road. Follow it .7 of a mile. Walk through the bridge to the site. (Pg 52, D5, Q4)
Parking: There is a small area on the left to park.
Swimming area: The large pool below the falls offers the deepest water for adults.

Visitor Guide:
Size & depth of pool: 3
No. & height of waterfalls: 4
Ease of location & access: 2
Uniqueness of features: 5

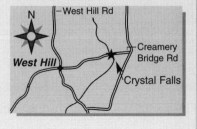

Eamon O'Shea goes head first into the main pool at Three Holes in Montgomery.

Three Holes

Upon the joining of the Jay and Wade Brook, Trout River starts just up stream from Three Holes. The headwater originates on Jay Peak and Hazens Notch. The combination of steep rises and high peaks makes this area extremely susceptible to flash floods.

On the east side of the main pool, a large boulder is the most popular hangout for swimmers. The rock offers a great overall view of the main pool's six-foot waterfall.

The most accessible and elegant waterfall, east of the lowest pool, fills the entire pool with a din. The cascading waterfall from the Hannah Clark Brook joins the Trout River at the main pool.

The second pool up, filled by an eight-foot waterfall, is completely hidden from the lower pool. The hemlocks on the west side of the hole have been washed away opening this pool up to the sun. The waterfall has worn a wide chute into the bedrock.

The upper waterfall is the largest falls of the four mentioned. It drops approximately eleven feet.

The uppermost pool is the most private but is dangerous due to its proximity to the falls. A large overhanging rock spur to the east of the upper pool is worth visiting.

Directions: Take Route 242 in Montgomery Center .2 of a mile to a long drive on the right with a large parking lot in the back. The old Montgomery school house was located here. A trail works its way east through the woods. (Pg 52, E6, Q2)

Parking: Park in the back lot near the woods.

Swimming area: The main pool is the first pool you will come to. Others are hard to reach.

Visitor Guide:

Size & depth of pool: 5

No. & height of waterfalls: 5

Ease of location & access: 3

Uniqueness of features: 4

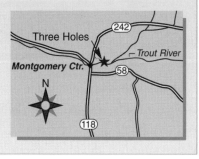

The calm tranquil pools at the Gibou Road swimming hole in Montgomery are the most private of any in the state.

34 / gibou road

Gibou Road

A crescent beach near the main pool at Gibou Road provides ample area for sunbathers. A channel connects the pool to the waterfalls and actually goes underneath a vaulted rock. The bubbling sound of the main falls echoes under here above the usual roar of the waterfall. A boulder blocks the main path to the falls and actually causes a dangerous rip current, so don't try to swim past here.

The stream rises over ten feet during the spring. On the east side of the stream, the bank is stripped clean of topsoil and the bedrock carved smooth.

The largest waterfall plunges six feet straight down.

Before leaving, take time to explore the covered bridge. The trusses inside the bridge are still covered with the advertisements that helped pull residents of Montgomery together as a community by informing them of important events.

The Gibou swimming hole is one of the most private of the area. Most locals prefer the more centrally located holes in town. It is not uncommon to see moose tracks along the roads.

Directions: Take Route 118 in Montgomery Center west to Eden. Take the second right, onto Gibou Road, after you leave the center. Drive about .2 of a mile until you see the Gibou Road covered bridge. A trail that looks like a four-wheeler path leads to the swimming hole on the south side of the bridge. (Pg 52, F6, Q2)

Parking: Park before the bridge on the left.

Swimming area: The best swimming is above the covered bridge in the main pool.

Seasonal runoff, however, deposits large amounts of sediment causing a fluctuation in pool depth.

Visitor Guide:

Size & depth of pool: 3

No. & height of waterfalls: 3

Ease of location & access: 3

Uniqueness of features: 3

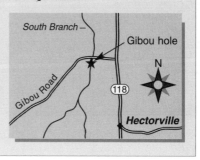

Swimmers are treated to a large natural waterfall at Four Corners in Troy.

Four Corners

Judging by the size of the parking area and the number of cars found in it, Four Corners is one of the top five most popular swimming holes in the state.

Like Montgomery, Troy wasn't blessed with a lake or pond for swimming. Residents of both areas have found a more than suitable alternative in the cool, clean mountain streams that pass through their towns.

A large portion of the eastern drainage of the Jay mountain chain passes through Four Corners on its way to the Missisquoi River, northern Vermont's 86-mile-long tributary to Lake Champlain that starts in Lowell and flows north.

A seven-foot waterfall, the centerpiece of the swimming hole, pumps water through the large main pool with fluid ripples. A steep ledge on the west side of the main pool is the most popular spot to sit. Here, the falls are the loudest due to the echo off the high cliffs that border the pool to the east.

Large rocks and trees often block and reflect the sound of the main falls. When this occurs, the lower falls are audible. This is a great example of how hard it is to pinpoint the source of a sound in the woods due to the reflection and absorption of sound waves.

Upstream from the main pool, a six-foot cascading waterfall and a narrow pool suffice for those who come to sunbathe and only need a little water to cool off.

Directions: Take Route 101 north from Lowell. Four Corners is less than a mile from Route 242 and across from a store called Four Corners. (Pg 53, B11, Q1)
Parking: Park across from the store in the large lot.
Swimming area: Most people swim below the main waterfall in the large pool. There are smaller more private pools upstream.

Visitor Guide:
Size & depth of pool: 5
No. & height of waterfalls: 4
Ease of location & access: 5
Uniqueness of features: 4

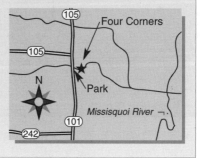

Emerald pools, high cliffs and a splashy waterfall among the few of the attractions at Cady Falls.

38 / cady falls

Cady Falls

Walking to the gorge one begins to wonder if this is what is meant by a wild goose chase. Anticipating a swimming hole bigger than the one you find is always disappointing.

But Cady Falls won't disappoint. The swimming hole is like a setting in a romantic painting. At the base of a 10-foot-wide waterfall, steep ridges and towering hemlocks rise 60 feet to form a needle canopy. Only in nature can the canvas be this large.

Perhaps the finest feature of Cady Falls is the waterfall, which drops twice to form a cascading seven-foot falls. The second falls shoots water outward in a fine spray. The splashy sound of the falls fills the entire cove. No where is that sound more apparent than from the top of the rock that adjoins the falls. Most of the sound is reflected up from the central pool.

Above the main falls, a steep walled chasm is home to a dark shallow pool. The green fuzzy moss-covered rock seems to be alive. When the wind passes though the channel the rock breathes.

Directions: Take Stagecoach Road .9 of a mile north from the Morristown General Store. You must hike about a mile through the woods. Upon entering the canopy, the trail splits. Bear to the left and head southeastward. Follow the trail until it reaches the water. The trail crosses the water and follows the brook upstream. (Pg 46, D6, Q3)

Parking: The pull off is on the left by two big boulders near the forest edge.

Swimming area: The large pool below the falls offers the best swimming. There are many other small holes above and below the falls that are nice for wading and swimming.

Visitor Guide:
Size & depth of pool: 5
No. & height of waterfalls: 3
Ease of location & access: 1
Uniqueness of features: 5

A boulder jammed in the Jeff Falls helps to deepen the shallow pool behind it.

Jeff Falls

Like blown glass with air bubbles, the rocky bank along the Brewster River has a globular look. Quarts deposits, comparable to drips of paint on a concrete floor, ornament these rounded features.

You won't want to miss the twin lower falls just below the parking lot where the water moves through a series of dips before being pushed out and up by the force behind it. To notice this scooping waterfall, the stream needs to be at normal flow. The two waterfalls fill the lower pool and account for the frothy sound near the pool.

A short walk upstream, at the base of a nearly seven-foot falls, lies the best pool for swimming. On sunny days the combination of greenish-blue rock and algae create an emerald pool so inviting that not even the most dedicated fisherman could resist.

A popular trout hole, the pool is oxygen rich from the waterfall as well as cool from the depth. It is common to see eight-inch trout in this pool. It is uncommon, however, to see someone catch one.

A sandy beach on the east side of the pool is in open light from about noon to 4 p.m. A large overhanging rock, with enough ceiling area to cover two large automobiles, rest on the bank south of the beach.

Directions: Take Route 108 south from Jeffersonville about .4 of a mile. There are two main paths to the water. The lower path brings you to the lower falls. The upper path brings you to the upper falls and pool.(Pg 46, B1, Q2)
Parking: There is a small pull off on the left with room for four cars.
Swimming area: The upper pool offers excellent swimming.

Visitor Guide:
Size & depth of pool: 3
No. & height of waterfalls: 4
Ease of location & access: 5
Uniqueness of features: 4

Genevieve Tamasik works her horse through Brewster Gorge in Jeffersonville. Vermont Horse Park guides riders to the park.

Brewster Gorge

A gorge, covered bridge, swimming hole, large aspen and short hike all await travelers who make their way to Brewster River Gorge Park to experience the unique natural features and great atmosphere.

The qualities that make this swimming hole a little different are the large aspen trees that compliment the waterfall in a saccharin symphony. Both take center stage during the year. The aspen resonate during the fall, and the waterfall, during the spring.

Just above the aspens the stream widens. This part of the swimming area has become a popular spot to bring dogs to fetch balls.

To the North of the lower swimming area, Scott Bridge, a nearly 85-foot-long lattice structure, spans the Brewster River.

Two boulders mark the main trail to the gorge. There are plenty of places to explore on the short hike to the falls. When you reach the gorge, don't be surprised if you don't see water, because it is hidden by the large boulders wedged in the gorge.

At the top of the gorge, over 40 trees, mostly hemlocks, are wedged in the channel. Many diving birds use these trees to watch for small trout trapped in the inner gorge pools.

Directions: Take Route 108 from Jeffersonville less than a mile to Canyon Road. Brewster Gorge is on the immediate right. The trail to the gorge runs parallel to the stream and crosses over it before leading to the falls. (Pg 46, B1, Q4)
Parking: Park in the lot.
Swimming area: The main swimming area is near the parking lot.

Visitor Guide:
Size & depth of pool: 3
No. & height of waterfalls: 5
Ease of location & access: 3
Uniqueness of features: 5

Megan Lovell and Jonathan Merrey get caught up in the romance of Bingham Falls.

Bingham Falls

Close your eyes a minute and imagine the most inviting pool with a single waterfall in the middle of paradise. Chances are you imagined a tranquil spot on a tropical island where everyone and everything is beautiful.

Although Bingham Falls cannot boast that, it is out of this world when it comes to Vermont. The originator of the phrase *Vermont is for lovers* no doubt swam here with his special someone during courtship.

The main attraction is the lower pool, which rests at a bend in the West Branch Waterbury River. The water has carved a cavity in the rock that makes the pool appear to be vaulted by hemlock trees.

A 12-foot waterfall fills the pool and is often the only area of the pool lit by the sun due to the dense hemlock canopy. Afternoon light reflects off the white water illuminating the dark rounded fissure.

The outlet of the pool has been carved into a narrow chute. The sloping rocks are perfect for sunbathing here. Don't expect much privacy. This is the most popular spot of the falls.

The many other falls have diverse characteristics. Some drop through narrow chutes, while others spray out over the bedrock and others still are scooped up into the air.

Directions: Take Route 108 from Jeffersonville over the notch. As you head down the mountain, Bingham Falls is on the left side, 10.3 miles from Jeffersonville or about a mile below the toll road in Stowe. (Pg 46, F3, Q1)

Parking: Parking is on both sides of the road near the Bingham Falls sign.

Swimming area: The only swimming area is at the base of the lowest and biggest waterfall.

Visitor Guide:

Size & depth of pool: 5
No. & height of waterfalls: 5
Ease of location & access: 5
Uniqueness of features: 5

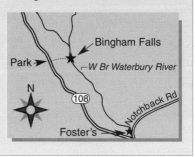

Calm waters and a nice stone wall make Foster's a popular swimming hole on weekends.

Foster's

The size of the swimming hole isn't always a good indicator of its popularity. Foster's is an example of this. Although to most it would seem less than a suitable alternative to a pond or lake, to residents of Stowe, it is a place as cherished as the mountains that form its headwater.

To say that Foster's is any less of a swimming hole than others would be to take the argument that the rock that one sits on is more important than the view. Of course the rock has little to do with the view, and so Stowe residents believe that swimming here is similar to the view — swimming is swimming no matter where you do it.

If you're looking for glorious waterfalls pass up Foster's. The only waterfall here is a three-foot cascade.

What makes this place unique is the stonewall on the south side of the pool. The wall is great for sunbathing, relaxing and picnicking. The sun hits the wall most of the afternoon.

Adjacent to the pool to the northwest, a mature hemlock stand has retarded growth on the forest floor. The pine siskin and red-breasted nuthatch seek out these sections of the forest. If you sit long enough a flicker will catch your eye. The birds create an interesting visual diversion from the brook.

Directions: Take Notchback Road (across from the Madahorn and adjacent to Foster's Place) .25 of a mile to a parking spot on the right. Notchback road is 1.3 miles south of Bingham Falls and 4.8 miles from Route 100 in Stowe. (Pg 46, F3, Q3)

Parking: Parking is minimal. There is a small parking area on the right.

Swimming area: The deepest and nicest pool is below the waterfall. A stonewall next to the pool is great for relaxing.

Visitor Guide:
Size & depth of pool: 3
No. & height of waterfalls: 2
Ease of location & access: 4
Uniqueness of features: 3

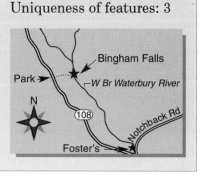

Stephanie Cunningham and Chris Hodgeman listen to the powerful falls from the trail overlook at Moss Glen Falls in Stowe.

48 / moss glen falls (stowe)

Moss Glen Falls *(Stowe)*

Vermont boasts two spectacular waterfalls with the name Moss Glen Falls. Stowe's version of the falls perhaps better epitomizes the nature of Vermont because it offers a view of the high peaks common to the state.

As visitors walk up the trail near the falls, the hemlocks thin as the chin of Mount Mansfield fills the skyline. A horizon dominated by this long mountain is a perfect backdrop for the over 80-foot waterfall.

The swimming hole at the base of the falls offers an excellent view of the waterfall as it makes its way over a section of knobby rock that splits the water in several channels. These channels exponentially split, creating a wide, wispy waterfall over 30-feet wide in places.

The stream cavity near the swimming hole dwarfs the largest man. The girth of the waterfall, the overhanging spur, and the tilting hemlocks create a dome 200 feet above the water.

Walking up the trail above the swimming hole to the height of the falls gives a unique perspective of the waterfall. The falls seem smaller because they not only rise but they also descend. The flume with several falls creates a cycling cacophony, because the water is pushed over in stages.

Directions: Take Route 100 north from Stowe about 3.2 miles to Randolph Road. Take a right onto Randolph Road and follow it .4 of a mile. Take a right onto Moss Glen Falls Road and follow it .5 of a mile until the road turns sharply. You will see the sign for the falls at the corner. (Pg 46, G6, Q3)
Parking: Park in the lot.
Swimming area: The pool below the falls offers a nice place to cool off. *Don't try to* *reach the inner gorge pools!*
Visitor Guide:
Size & depth of pool: 1
No. & height of waterfalls: 5
Ease of location & access: 4
Uniqueness of features: 5

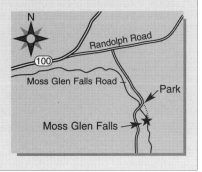

At Sheep's Hole everything seems to lead to the main falls. The pool is wading level, making it a great place to bring children.

Sheep's Hole

Located near Johnson State College, this swimming hole is a popular spot for many students familiar with the area. This spot is perhaps the smallest swimming hole covered in this book, but it is by no means the least desirable place to visit.

The strong points of this swimming hole are moss layers, privacy, proximity to the Long Trail, a stone wall and elegant waterfalls.

The cascading four-foot waterfall that fills the pool fits the pool's character. The smooth flowing waterfall cuts under a rock and works against the grain of the stream before filling the shallow pool.

Two-hundred-year-old moss covers many of the rocks higher on the bank. The moss is a good indicator of the last flood that was high enough to wash the rock surface clean.

Shaded nearly all day, the hole is part of the Foot Brook, a small waterway carrying water from Butternut Mountain.

The Long Trail carries hikers several hundred feet above Sheep's Hole. The terrain is rugged and relatively high when compared to other swimming holes. The elevation is the limiting factor to the amount of water flowing down the brook.

Directions: Take Clay Hill Road in the center of Johnson approximately 2 miles to Plot Cemetery Road. This road is not marked. From Johnson, it is the third road on the left. Take a left onto Plot Cemetery Road and go .8 of a mile. The road will fork, so stay to the left and then turn left where the road seems to end. The swimming hole is on the left near the intersection. (Pg 46, A4, Q2)

Parking: Park on the left side of the road.

Swimming area: The pool is below the falls.

Visitor Guide:

Size & depth of pool: 2
No. & height of waterfalls: 2
Ease of location & access: 2
Uniqueness of features: 4

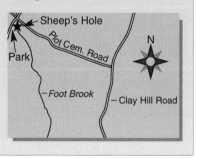

The broken dam at The Mill has become an accepted part of the landscape in Worcester and a relished swimming hole to residents.

The Mill

The Mill is the site of an old dam, long since washed away by spring floods. It is part of Minister Brook, which along with Patterson and Hancock brooks, is responsible for most of the eastern runoff of the Worcester Mountains.

Almost in the valley between the Worcester and Woodbury mountains, the swimming hole maintains much of its volume even during the summer.

Part of the dam overhangs the pool near the falls. Most of the south side of the dam is still intact and has become the drawing board for a few idle minds with spray cans.

One would tend to think that manmade structures take away from the natural wonder of a waterfall or swimming hole. This dam, however, seems to add a touch of character to the hole. The broken structure is a humbling example of man's attempt to harness the power of water.

A close look at the broken wall reveals some of the weaknesses that most likely contributed to the dam's functional destruction. The foundation of the wall seems to have separated from the dam itself.

The pool, deepest near the 11-foot waterfall, slowly becomes shallow until it reaches the outlet where stones have collected forming the bowl-like bottom.

Directions: Take Minister Brook Road, from Route 12 in Worcester, about .4 of a mile. A trail leads straight down from the road to the dam. A lower trail, a short walk down the road, leads to the main pool.
(Pg 47, K8, Q1)
Parking: There is room for only a couple of vehicles on the brook side of the road.
Swimming area: The main pool is just below the falls.

Visitor Guide:
Size & depth of pool: 4
No. & height of waterfalls: 4
Ease of location & access: 3
Uniqueness of features: 4

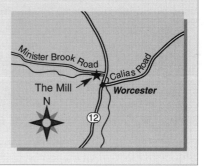

Bolton Potholes is a study in geology. The potholes have been created by the fast moving water that flows down the Joiner Brook.

Bolton Potholes

Water carrying hard stones formed the bowls known as Bolton Potholes. Each hole, like a fish ladder, rises incrementally above the pool below it. Although only a small amount of water flows down the Joiner Brook into the pools, they are deep enough to maintain most of their volume even when the narrow chutes filling the pools begin to dry up.

The upper pool is the most narrow of the four steps. It is deep enough to swim in comfortably and is great for dogs that like to swim and fetch tennis balls. Of the pools, this one offers the most privacy.

The water begins to tumble over the five waterfalls from the upper pool. Walking southward from the pool, swimmers climb the highest open face of the rock.

The most popular bowl, the bottom middle pool abuts a ledge to the east. Access to this pool is from the west.

The lowest pool is also the largest. A stony beach remains sun-swept long after sloping rockface.

The rocks leading from pool to pool are very slippery. Many rocks are striated downward (from water) giving little grip when traveling in the same direction. The easiest way around the rocks is to backtrack toward the parking area and walk down the west side.

Directions: Take Route 2 about 6.6 miles from Waterbury. Take a right onto Bolton Valley Road. The holes are about .25 of a mile up the hill on the right. (Pg 45, K14, Q2)

Parking: Park off the traveled portion of the road for safety and to avoid being ticketed or towed.

Swimming area: The bottom pool offers a variety of depths for all ages and the large middle pool (the second lowest pool) is nice for adults when water flow is minimal.

Visitor Guide:
Size & depth of pool: 5
No. & height of waterfalls: 5
Ease of location & access: 5
Uniqueness of features: 5

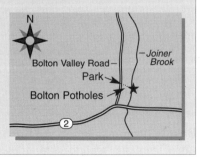

Brenda Rogowski enjoys the fine spray of the New Haven River as it drops over the main falls at Bristol Falls.

Bristol Falls

The New Haven River boasts some of the largest and most popular swimming holes in the state. Home to Bristol Falls and Circle Current, this river's tributaries drain mountains in Addison, Chittenden and Washington Counties. Summertime heat draws visitors from over 30 miles away. On hot days as many as 200 people scatter among the trees and pools.

The main pool is the draw of the area. It is the second pull off up the hill on the right. The rocks near the large upper pool are slanted as if to provide the best angle for laying out in the summer sun. The pool is so large it will seem like you are at a beach.

Only after entering the water do visitors notice that the bank where most visitors sit is undercut by the water, creating a spur.

The treat of this pool is the wide sheeted waterfall. When the water is low, some locals swim to the south side of the falls and climb over the slick rock to get under the falls. There is enough room to fit a large car under the falls.

From the waterfall, the water makes its way through a trough to a wide, shallow beach area. A smooth sloping rock to the south of the pool creates a buffer zone between the water and the forest.

Directions: From Route 116 in Bristol, take Lincoln Gap Road. After you turn, the lower section of the swimming areas is immediately to the right. The upper section is about .4 of a mile up. (Pg 39, H10, Q4)

Parking: Park in the lots to the right of the road.

Swimming area: The main pool at Bristol Falls is accessible from the lower part of the upper parking lot. The best swimming is in the large pool near the upper waterfall, but there are some great private pools below.

Visitor Guide:

Size & depth of pool: 5
No. & height of waterfalls: 5
Ease of location & access: 5
Uniqueness of features: 5

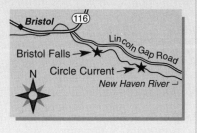

Less than a mile from Bristol Falls, Circle Current is big enough to accommodate a large number of visitors.

Circle Current

If you have ever been down a slide at a water park, you will experience *deja vu* here. The long narrow channels resemble the slides and sharp turns that you would find at many parks. The only difference is that these are rugged and potentially dangerous.

The only time to slide is in July or August when the water flow is low. The water here is forced around several natural stone dams. The dams run parallel to each other and create a gutter between them where water can flow. The water runs perpendicular to the river and then makes a sharp turn near the river's edge.

In a few places, it is possible to turn with the water to go down the next little gutter.

Before you attempt to slide, ask someone nearby if they have ever slid there and where the best place to slide is. If you are lucky you may even get a demonstration. Don't let children try it however.

The most popular part of this swimming area is the pool just above the series of chutes. The sediment deposits here fluctuate slightly but are never so substantial that the swimming is limited.

A secluded, sandy beach near the parking lot is the best area to spread out a towel to relax in the shade.

Directions: From Route 116 in Bristol, take Lincoln Gap Road about a mile (another .2 of a mile from the upper pull off for Bristol Falls). (Pg 39, H10, Q4)

Parking: Just past the swimming hole, park on the right.

Swimming area: There is a nice pool straight back from the parking lot that is the most private and the safest for children. The main pool with the long channels that cross the river is the most crowded.

Visitor Guide:

Size & depth of pool: 5

No. & height of waterfalls: 5

Ease of location & access: 5

Uniqueness of features: 5

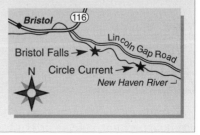

Christopher Chaloux measures the fish he almost caught in the strong current at Garland's Bridge.

Garland's Bridge

If privacy is what you're after, and if neighboring Circle Current and Bristol Falls are just a little too popular for your taste, then try this swimming hole. Garland's Bridge, with just enough space in the parking area for two vehicles, goes unnoticed by most travelers.

The deep narrow swimming hole has a stony beach, an ethereal waterfall and even a little elaborate art work on the bridge abutments. Adjacent to the art work, the old bridge abutments rest on a small ledge.

When they built the new steel bridge here they made new support structures and discarded the old ones by simply knocking them from their perch. Although this is a slight eyesore, the sight of them doesn't discredit the swimming hole.

The main pool is usually dammed with large stones by the local kids who swim here. This raises the water level. The lower pool, below the dam, is actually the largest (but not as inviting).

The water flows in between two large rocks near the lower pool Over time the water created a miniature gorge, which churns and froths like a gorge twice its size.

Directions: From Route 116 in Bristol, take Lincoln Gap Road about another 4 miles from Circle Current, or just over five miles from Route 116. The bridge is just before you reach the road to South Lincoln, which is on the right. (Pg 39, I12, Q3)

Parking: Park in the pull off on the left side of the road just after a steel bridge.

Swimming area: The deepest swimming area is below the bridge. There is also a lower pool below the northernmost waterfall.

Visitor Guide:

Size & depth of pool: 3
No. & height of waterfalls: 2
Ease of location & access: 5
Uniqueness of features: 2

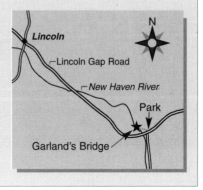

Brett Belknap does a flip at Warren Falls. This risky act should be
avoided by all visitors.

Warren Falls

Formed in the same way as the Bolton Potholes, Warren Falls is a good example of the large bowls that are created when harder stones are trapped in crevices of bedrock.

Four falls make up this dynamic swimming hole that occasionally draws several hundred visitors on humid summer days. A steep dropping four-foot waterfall is the first falls visitors see when walking to the pools. The water flows over the bedrock in a smooth even fashion, creating feathery white water. The next waterfall down is eroding the solid rock and is hard to see because of the narrow chasm it travels through. The west bank above the middle pools is steep and marked by a narrow trail.

Smooth sloping rocks characterize the east side of the swimming hole. Nearly all of the visitors spend their time on the east side of the hole on these rocks, open to the late day sun.

The middle upper pool has a unique double falls leaving the pool. The waterfalls fill a shallow pool below two ledges.

Many visitors who bring their dogs use the lowest pool. In the shade of the tall hemlocks on the steep west bank, the shallow pool and rocky beach near the outlet are less crowded and allow dogs some room to run.

Directions: From the Warren village outlet, travel 3 miles south on Route 100 to a large pull off on the right. A sign that reads 43rd Infantry Division Memorial Highway marks the lot. Follow the trail that bears to the right. (Pg 40, I1, Q3)
Parking: There is room for about 20 cars in lot.
Swimming area: The main pools for swimming are the lower pools. Some visitors also make use of the stream before the falls in the summer.

Visitor Guide:
Size & depth of pool: 5
No. & height of waterfalls: 5
Ease of location & access: 5
Uniqueness of features: 5

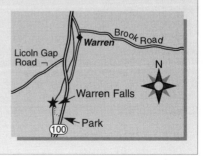

Nicole Laliberte nears the surface of the water at Pikes Falls after doing a shallow dive.

Southern Region

Swimming holes in the southern part of the state take on a different personality from their northern counterparts. Smaller and less frequent, southern swimming holes inspire images of quintessential early American life, when the town fishing hole was also the town swimming hole.

Children stopped along these streams to play and swim on warm spring days. Parents found their children splashing and playing in the cool pools.

These places became synonymous with carefree, exuberant times. As those children grew, they left the banks that held the gold to their childhood.

When the children return as adults to once again set eyes on the waterfalls, swim in the bone-chilling waters and sit on the stream banks to listen to nature's song, they reconnect the link to their childhood. Maybe the channels that carry the water downstream also carry visitors back to their childhood — back to their old swimming holes.

If you visit swimming holes in southern Vermont, you will see adults acting like children. And of course children acting like children. These places allow us to be ourselves. The cold water shocks us into feeling every ounce of our living being. The majestic chasms and powerful waterfalls awaken our sleeping souls to mortality.

A stranger across the way who looks up from a book once in a while to watch the breeze feather the leaves is experiencing life as a child. If you talk to that lone stranger, you might be surprised at the feeling of kinship you have with him.

Like tall hemlocks that stand side by side during their life to pass the days, so do strangers — whether they live 10 miles away or 1,000. In discovering our similarities we discover ourselves. As you discover these swimming holes, I'm sure that they will conjure up all sorts of feelings from your childhood. And I can promise that you will become part of the Earth here. This is plainly clear at Hamilton Falls, Pikes Falls and Twin Bridges — discover it for yourself.

With the arc from the bridge above, swimmers risk their safety by diving into the water below.

East Middlebury Gorge

The arch that was extensively used by the Romans to support their infrastructure is still around today. East Middlebury Gorge gives visitors the opportunity to inspect a modern arch while lazily floating on their backs.

The bridge that spans the Middlebury River above East Middlebury Gorge has its problems, but the arch remains solid, possibly delaying the construction of a new bridge.

The main swimming area at the gorge is a long deep channel with parallel stone walls on its edge. The large arch blocks much of the day's sun.

A series of flat steps that look like stacked pancakes meet the water to the north. These are great for sunbathing during the afternoon.

If you swim to the ten-foot cascading waterfall that feeds the channel, look at the fragmented rocks on the upstream side of the bridge near the falls. These rocks have been split and abraded causing many to pile along the water's edge. Few other swimming holes or waterfalls in the state offer such an unusual spectacle.

There are some smaller pools along the river that are great for swimming and fly fishing. Some pools fill with air bubbles making them great places to float and relax with friends.

Directions: From Route 7 near East Middlebury, take Route 125 about 1.5 miles to a sharp right-hand turn. Cross the bridge here. The path to the water is back across the bridge in the direction you came, on the left side of the road as you are walking. (Pg 33, C11, Q1)
Swimming area: Swim in the long channel below the bridge.
Parking: Park on the right side of the bridge after you cross it.

Visitor Guide:
Size & depth of pool: 5
No. & height of waterfalls: 4
Ease of location & access: 5
Uniqueness of features: 5

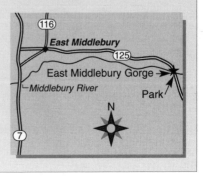

Vermont's finest qualities are evident in the Falls of Lana at Branbury State Park.

Falls of Lana

Once named Sucker Brook Falls, the Falls of Lana was renamed after General Wool in 1850. The name of the waterfall literally means falls of General Wool, since the Spanish word for wool is actually *lana*.

Located on the east side of Lake Dunmore, the Falls of Lana offers the most diverse views of any waterfall in the state. Trails lead to the bottom of the falls, to the sides, to the top and even to some of the interior waterway. From the eastern ledge of the falls, you can see Lake Dunmore.

The trail to the bottom of the falls is very steep and marked by loose rock. The lower outlook offers a view of the biggest waterfall. The falls split up over a lumpy series of rocks, creating a wide thin spray. The entire waterfall appears to be covered in green wool.

Most are content with seeing just the lower view of the waterfall. But there are two other falls that are hidden. Two sharp bends in the brook contribute to the secrecy.

If you walk along the trail to the top of the waterfall, you will see the other falls. Only by crossing the river well above the falls will you be able to see the other waterfalls up close.

Most visitors swim in the small pools a good distance up the stream from the falls.

Don't swim near the large waterfalls or in the inner pools!

Directions: From Route 7 in Salisbury, take Route 53, 3.8 miles to the Falls of Lana. The pull off is just past the entrance to Branbury State Park. From the lot, follow the trail a quarter of the mile to the waterfall.
(Pg 33, E10, Q2)

Parking: Parking is free at the pull off, but you have to pay at the state park.

Swimming area: There are nice pools several hundred feet above the falls.

Visitor Guide:
Size & depth of pool: 3
No. & height of waterfalls: 5
Ease of location & access: 4
Uniqueness of features: 5

Mark Lown, front, and his brother Cory enjoy a tube ride down the White River on a hot day in July.

Dean's Hill

The farther a person travels south the harder it is to find deep, heavy-volume swimming holes in mountain streams. Southern regions have an answer — river swimming. Located on the White River, Dean's Hill and Twin Bridges are the *creme de la creme* of river swimming in the state. Seldom will you find a river as clear and clean with such unique recreation.

Dean's Hill, located on a sharp bend in the river, is the first swimming hole reached during a tube ride down the White (see also Twin Bridges). The hole rests peacefully just outside of the Green Mountain National Forest, where many of the White's headwaters form.

Dean's Hill is just one of many calm pools. The white water on the hole's west side has helped establish the White River's reputation for fishing. The rapids above the swimming hole are loud enough to drown out the highway, yet, quite enough to provide a pleasant atmosphere for swimmers and fishermen.

The north side of the pool is great for sunbathing for most of the day. Some visitors come here for mud baths. On the south side, a stony beach is a popular picnic spot for swimmers early in the year.

The river current is deceivingly strong. Without even a ripple, water can pass downstream at over 5 mph. Swimming across the river quickly becomes an effort to swim upstream.

Directions: Go west on Route 107 about .3 of a mile from Gaysville. The trail to the water heads northwest down a steep enbankment. (Pg 34, I4, Q4)

Parking: Park on the right side of the road. There is room for about four cars.

Swimming area: The river is deep enough for swimming anywhere.

Visitor Guide:
Size & depth of pool: 4
No. & height of waterfalls: 4
Ease of location & access: 4
Uniqueness of features: 4

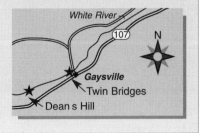

Also known as Lion's Head, Twin Bridges is a great stop on the White River.

Twin Bridges

If you want to have lots of fun, go to the Gaysville Trading Company and rent inner tubes for tubing down the White River. After renting tubes, leave a car near the Gaysville store and take another one west on Route 107. Turn right onto Route 100 and park at the steel bridge and tube down the White. On the way you will pass birds, deer and trout.

Depending on the current, it takes just over two hours to tube to Gaysville. After the trip take a car back to get the other vehicle up river.

If you only have the luxury of one vehicle, ask whoever is working at the store if any other groups are heading upstream who may want to car pool. You may even inquire at the local campground.

The Twin Bridges swimming area is west of the large steel bridge under the shade of a large rock known as Lion's Head. This is the deepest part of the river for several miles. The ledge runs northeast to support the bridge before it descends to a flat sandy beach. Beach access is available only to campers staying at the White River Valley Campground.

The bridge offers an excellent vantage point to view the White River Valley.

Directions: Twin Bridges is across from the Gaysville Trading Company store. It is approximately 6 miles from the three way intersection in Bethal. (Pg 34, I4, Q4)

Parking: The post office has posted signs in the past prohibiting parking on its premises. Park near the bridge.

Swimming area: People swim on the west side of the bridge and tube down the river. The west rocks are great for relaxing.

Visitor Guide:

Size & depth of pool: 5
No. & height of waterfalls: 4
Ease of location & access: 5
Uniqueness of features: 5

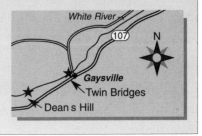

The Narrows is a nearly perfect stop on a hot summer day when the nearby lake is crowded.

The Narrows

Characterized by the long slender channel that runs under the steel bridge, The Narrows symbolizes the essence of every small backwoods swimming hole in the state.

Locust Creek changes from a shallow meandering creek to a tiny gorge, which is filled by a three-foot waterfall.

What made the conditions right to create this hole is largely subjective. But the steep walled ledge adjacent to the bridge suggests a break in the bedrock allowed the water to pass through. Overtime, the water smoothed the ledge walls and deepened the channel as it sped up to pass through the narrow passage.

Even today as the water makes its way out of the channel it is changing the creek bed as it makes a sharp turn. Just downstream from The Narrows, the creek, less than a foot deep in most places, meanders as it did upstream before the hole.

This is an excellent hole to bring children to watch trout, suckers and dace feed. To see the fish, stay out of the water and sit on the sloping rock on the west side of the creek. On clear days, the fish will swim in and out of the sunlight, making them easy to see.

The landowner has nailed a sign to a tree asking visitors to treat the land with respect. Let us make sure we do.

Directions: From Route 107 in Bethal take Route 12 south .5 of a mile. Take a right onto Old Creek Road. Go about .2 of a mile until you pass a steel bridge. Walk back in the direction you came to reach the water. (Pg 34, I5, Q2)
Parking: Park after the bridge on the right.
Swimming area: The hole is below the bridge in the long narrow channel.

Visitor Guide:
Size & depth of pool: 3
No. & height of waterfalls: 2
Ease of location & access: 3
Uniqueness of features: 2

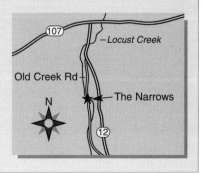

One could spend a lifetime walking the Earth and never find a group
of waterfalls more majestic and peaceful than the ones in Mendon.

McLaughlin Falls

If you've tried other swimming holes and have been a little disappointed by the amount of people at them, you may want to try this swimming hole. Although McLaughlin Falls is a very popular spot for swimmers, weekdays are a little more quiet.

If you plan to swim at McLaughlin Falls, leave a little extra time to inspect the series of waterfalls. Few natural areas in Vermont can boast of more delicate and elegant cascades, plunges and trickles than McLaughlin Falls.

In addition to the falls, the inner pools near the upper waterfall are prime examples of how bowls form in the bedrock. Stones, harder than the bedrock, are deposited in the bowls and circulate in the pool. These erosive stones act as nature's sandpaper, wearing away the bedrock.

As a result of this circular current, bowled and cratered formations dominate the middle pools. When the water is low, many visitors swim in the middle pool where the waterfall drops out over the lower bedrock. This area provides a nice space under the falls to explore. This middle pool is parallel to a stone wall, with trees over 40 years old growing from it. From the middle bowls, the water flows through a cascading seven-foot waterfall before forming a 12-foot waterfall that drops into a pool adjacent to a rocky beach that is excellent for sunbathing.

Directions: From Route 4 in Mendon, take Wheelerville Road 5 miles to bridge 15. A trail before the bridge on the left leads to the swimming hole. (Pg 29, D14, Q1)

Parking: Park either before or after the bridge on the left. Be sure to stay off the road.

Swimming area: The main swimming hole is in the biggest pool below the 12-foot waterfall.

Visitor Guide:
Size & depth of pool: 3
No. & height of waterfalls: 5
Ease of location & access: 2
Uniqueness of features: 4

The rock formations at Devil's Gorge are as impressive as the long
deep channel.

Devil's Gorge

When you walk into this gorge for the first time, there is a strange sensation that you just may be walking into the Devil's Gorge. The steep bank to the water provides a challenging obstacle to escape, and the tight-walled gorge provides the security of a lair.

With twin 33-foot ledges on the north and south sides, Devil's Gorge is one of the narrowest gorges in the state. The water that flows through the gorge has shaped and molded the stone into crude pieces of art. The centerpiece of this rock carving exhibit is a mushroom shaped rock on the north side of the river near the end of the nearly 110-foot channel.

Even the color of the rock sculptures looks painted on. The rocks on the south side of the river are strangely luminescent. The warm morning sun appears to be hitting the curved edges of a few of these rocks. Even on the most cloudy day these strange rocks will tell your mind the sun is shining from the east.

The main channel itself appears calm, but the narrow passage actually forces the water to move faster. This is only apparent when you go for a swim. The inlet to the channel is a cascading 6-foot waterfall that is difficult to reach unless you are a strong swimmer and can swim to it.

Directions: From Route 7 in Clarendon take Gorge Road, east of Route 7. Gorge Road is the same turn as Route 7B. Go about 1.9 miles. The trail to the water is on the right and can be steep and hazardous when it is wet. (Pg 29, G13, Q3)

Parking: There is a small pull off on the right, just after a horseback riding sign.

Swimming area: The swimming hole is the long narrow channel below the waterfall.

Visitor Guide:
Size & depth of pool: 4
No. & height of waterfalls: 3
Ease of location & access: 3
Uniqueness of features: 3

John Lambert lets go of a rope at the end of a swing before diving into the Mill River. Don't try this!

Clarendon Gorge

Flowing through a high-walled gorge, Mill River in Clarendon supports most of the swimming in the area. The river's headwaters form miles south of Clarendon in the Green Mountain National Forest in Wallingford. One of many tributaries to Otter Creek, Mill River winds a serpentine path through the foothills to get here.

The lower Clarendon Gorge, with its wide deep channel and pebble beach, can draw as many as 30 people on humid summer days.

Lacking the waterfalls that make other swimming holes popular, the lower Clarendon Gorge's beauty lies in its deep pools.

The main pool is bordered on the south by a rocky knoll that rolls back away from the water. To the west, the Mill River Bridge, part of Route 7, is just 40 yards away. Just above the pool the river bends 45 degrees north. The water upstream is nearly impossible to reach from the chasm edge.

The increase in popularity of the lower swimming hole has resulted in the blocking of the road to the gorge in order to prevent overnight camping and visitors from driving vehicles on the steep banks near the water. The swimming hole, as a result of abusive actions, is only open during the day.

This swimming hole will present each of us with opportunities to leave it better than we found it.

Directions: From Route 7 in Clarendon, take Gorge Road, east of Route 7. Gorge Road is the same turn as Route 7B. Once you turn, immediately take the first right. (Pg 29, G13, Q3)
Parking: There is a pull off marked by several concrete barriers.
Swimming area: The swimming hole is just up the blocked road to the left.

Visitor Guide:
Size & depth of pool: 4
No. & height of waterfalls: 1
Ease of location & access: 4
Uniqueness of features: 2

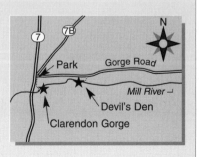

Walking across swinging bridge can be a frightening and disorienting experience, even to the most steel-nerved visitor.

Swinging Bridge

Swinging Bridge is the only swimming hole that can boast a suspended bridge, a hike on the Long Trail and a walk to the water that is just as fun as the swim.

The swimming hole to the south of the bridge offers the best swimming. The worn trail to the water is very steep, so go farther downstream for safer entry to the swimming hole.

The gorge narrows at the swimming hole, which rests just downstream of a sharp turn in the river. To get there, visitors must cross a 60 foot bridge. Upon stepping onto the expanse, one understands why the swimming hole is called swinging bridge.

If you look downstream from the middle of the bridge, you can see how deep the gorge is, since the surrounding forest conceals the gorge by draping its edges in a canopy.

Upstream from the bridge, campsites dot the forest floor within yards of the water. The streamside location, with the quiet sound of running water, serves as a night refuge for hikers on the Long Trail.

The river near the campsites is wide and full of boulders. It's possible to walk across or down the river hopping from rock to rock during the summer. Try this and you will surely see the small dace and trout swim from under many of the rocks you step on.

Directions: From Route 7, take Route 103, 2.5 miles to a large parking lot. Follow the path across the river on the suspended bridge.
(Pg 29, G13, Q3)

Parking: There is room for 20 cars in the large parking lot on the right side of the road.

Swimming area: People swim on both sides of the of the suspended bridge. Some upper pools are more private.

Visitor Guide:

Size & depth of pool: 3
No. & height of waterfalls: 3
Ease of location & access: 3
Uniqueness of features: 4

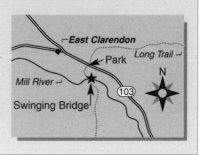

Buttermilk Falls has become known for its large waterfalls, making it one of Vermont's most popular swimming holes.

Buttermilk Falls

When first visiting Buttermilk Falls, most people miss one of the waterfalls. They usually feel like they have discovered the swimming hole everyone has been talking about. But the thing to remember about Buttermilk Falls is that there are two very similar swimming holes on the brook not more than 150 yards apart. The wide, 14-foot lower waterfall drops into a wide, deep pool and so does the top waterfall. And both have an impressive bedrock wall that the water flows over to the west of the swimming holes.

The two major differences between the two is that the upper swimming hole has a cascading waterfall, whereas the lower waterfall drops sharply. The upper one also has a rock step on the north side of the pool that people use for sunbathing. If visitors actually find both of these, they seldom are lucky enough to discover the most private swimming hole of them all — a third hole upstream near Route 103.

On hot days people cool off by sitting in their lawn chairs in the shallow part of the upper most pool.

Remember to carry out your trash. Don't be confused by the overflowing trash containers. They are rarely changed and almost always overflowing. Help keep the garbage here under control.

Directions: From Route 103 (near the junction of Route 100), take Buttermilk Falls Road to the end. The pools are on the right side of the road. (Pg 30, J4 Q1)

Parking: Park off the end of the road.

Swimming area: The two main pools are located below the upper and lower waterfalls. A third swimming area, at the very end of Buttermilk Falls Road, has a nice pool but no waterfall.

Visitor Guide:

Size & depth of pool: 5
No. & height of waterfalls: 5
Ease of location & access: 5
Uniqueness of features: 5

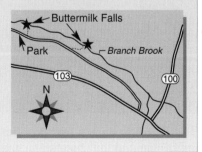

The Ottauquechee River has carved a deep gorge in the Vermont landscape making Quechee Gorge a must see.

Quechee Gorge

Renowned as Vermont's little grand canyon, Quechee Gorge is one of the state's most popular tourist stops. At 165-feet deep and over a mile long, Quechee Gorge is a must see in anyone's book.

Before hiking the trails or swimming at the bottom of the gorge, get a map from the Quechee Chamber of Commerce. The map has specialty shops, hiking trails, picnic areas and landmarks on it.

To really appreciate the gorge walk out onto the gorge bridge. The view south and north is great for photography whether taking stills or video. Notice how the gorge forms a V-shaped indentation in the earth creating a natural waterway. The trail along the gorge goes under the bridge to give visitors a sense of the gorge's width.

The swimming area is in the Ottauquechee River downstream of the bridge where the gorge flattens out and the channel splits. Swimmers take the trail leading to the bottom.

Both the channel and the wider outlet pools offer excellent swimming. Depending on the amount of rain, water clarity changes, so swimmers should be prepared to go somewhere else if they encounter dirty water.

Directions: Quechee Gorge is 5 miles from White River Junction and 6 miles from Woodstock. The trail to the water is west of the parking lot. Follow the trail under the bridge and down the hill to the lower swimming area. (Pg 31, C11, Q3)
Parking: The parking lot is on the northeast side of the road near the gifts and sportswear shops.
Swimming area: The only pools are on the downstream side of the gorge.
Visitor Guide:
Size & depth of pool: 5
No. & height of waterfalls: 5
Ease of location & access: 5
Uniqueness of features: 5

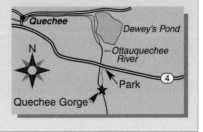

The rock sculptures at many swimming holes welcome visitors by letting them know that they are not alone.

Twenty Foot

When hearing the name Twenty Foot, most imagine a waterfall the name should describe. Going to this swimming hole expecting a large waterfall is a little disappointing. Fortunately, the pools for which the name describes are just as pleasurable.

Two flumes, with deep pools for their size, are hidden beneath a hemlock haven, 150 feet from the road and completely concealed from pedestrians.

The North Branch Black River flows east and collects in these large pools. One is directly below the parking area and offers an enjoyable swim to a cascading waterfall. The other is about 150-feet downstream. Both have pools that expand slightly at falls and then maintain a wide long channel.

Walking to the water reveals several clues as to how the terrain has been eroded. Much of the fragmented rock on the ground has been broken by water that freezes and expands in the crevasses. Hemlock roots follow the crevasses in search of water. As the roots grow they also help to break apart the rock.

Without these cracks, the trees couldn't maintain their grip in the shallow topsoil. This process is evident along the banks of the pool where many roots are left exposed.

(If there are more than two cars at this swimming hole, visit on another day.)

Directions: From Route 106 in Reading (Fletchville), take South Reading Road exactly 1 mile to a pine cone covered pull off on the left. Go left over the hill. (Pg 31, I8, Q3)

Parking: The pull off is across from a gray house. Park on the left side of the road and make sure all four wheels are off the pavement.

Swimming area: Two 20-foot pools are great for swimming.

Visitor Guide:

Size & depth of pool: 3
No. & height of waterfalls: 2
Ease of location & access: 3
Uniqueness of features: 3

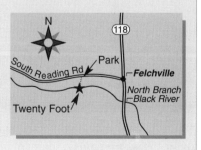

Tim Clouart slides down Mill Brook on the slippery algae covered rocks. *Don't try this.*

The Water Slide

Sliding down the rocks at The Water Slide would be a real nail-biting experience if your hands and arms weren't tensed and rigid from sheer terror. Watch the locals as they slide over and over and notice that the fear never leaves them.

Some exceed speeds of 20 mph before they are pushed off a three-foot waterfall into the main pool. The fast moving water, smooth rock, generous slope and algae all make for a fast, slick ride.

Although it is tempting to slide after watching someone, resist the urge. *The slide can be dangerous — especially in the spring when debris collects in the main pool.*

The slide is part of one of the most beautiful cascading waterfalls in the state.

Walking on the stream bed can be difficult. The sides all slant toward the center of the stream, which forms an angular funnel.

Avoid this swimming hole when the outer rock becomes wet from dew or rain. The slick algae found in the pools and along the stream tends to stick to feet making walking hazardous.

Nowhere will you find a place that allows you to walk along a grade that drops 35 feet within so short a distance.

Directions: From Route 7 in Danby take Mt. Tabor Avenue to Main Street. Take a right onto Main Street and go approximately .1 of a mile. Take a left onto Brook Road and go .1 of a mile. (Pg 25, B11, Q2)

Parking: Park on the left side of the road and obey the parking signs.

Swimming area: The only pool for swimming is located at the bottom of the cascading waterfall.

Visitor Guide:
Size & depth of pool: 3
No. & height of waterfalls: 5
Ease of location & access: 3
Uniqueness of features: 5

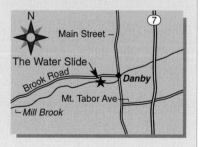

Nicole Beebe practices her drum while Will Clingenpeel takes a dip in the lower pool at Benson's Hole.

Benson's Hole

Named after the landowner, Benson's Hole exhibits the best of Southern-Vermont-style swimming holes.

What makes this hole unique is its proximity to 3,852-foot Equinox Mountain, which seems to rise straight up from Manchester Valley.

The rounded amber bedrock here is very common in Southern Vermont. The bedrock takes on a special look near streams. Moss, thriving in a moist cool air, fills the cracks in the bedrock, making it appear to have veins.

Two pools, one just below Route 7 and the other below Glen Road Bridge, are the fixtures here. Filled by a cascading waterfall with falls of over eight feet, the upper fan-shaped pool rests below a bathtub-sized Jacuzzi that provides a tingly bath. The entire pool fills with bubbles that are swept over another falls.

The lower pool is excellent for swimming, even though it is shallow in most places. The rocks are the best spots to tan. On hot summer days musicians practice, in harmony with nature's song, along this river.

Directions: From Route 30 (AKA Route 11), take East Manchester Road 1.1 miles to Glen Road. Turn left onto Glen Road. The trail to the swimming hole is on the west side of Glen Road Bridge. (Pg 25, H11, Q3)
Parking: Park before the bridge on the right.
Swimming area: Two pools offer nice swimming. The first is located just below Glen Road bridge. The other is located near the Route 7 bridge. Both pools are relatively shallow throughout.
Visitor Guide:
Size & depth of pool: 3
No. & height of waterfalls: 3
Ease of location & access: 3
Uniqueness of features: 3

Betsy Didan tries to coax a frog into her hands at Salmon Hole on the West River.

Salmon Hole

Salmon Hole is located inside Jamaica State Park. It is the site of the historic "Salmon Hole Massacre" of 1748.

Soldiers, who were in retreat from a band of Indians, were ambushed at Salmon Hole as they shot fish to eat. The soldiers retreated and were chased.

Captain Eleazer Melvin, the leader of the soldiers, escaped only by pointing an empty gun at his pursuers. In his journal, he describes being narrowly missed by several bullets. The captain returned days later with 40 men to bury the dead.

Six soldiers died in this battle known as King George's War. Today the chaos of a life and death battle is only a figment of visitors' imaginations as they make their way across the sandy shore to the pool. Children are the only ones trying to capture living things here anymore. And frogs are most often the target.

There are two swimming holes in the park. The other is aptly named Salmon Hole 2. Both holes offer bountiful fishing and are located at the bottom of a set of rocky rapids.

The river runs through a steep gorge that gives you the impression that you are really part of the mountains. If you want to camp, you will want to call ahead for reservations. The park is one of the most popular in the state and books up for the holidays early in the year.

Directions: Take Depot St .4 of a mile to Jamaica State Park. Ask for a map of the park at the ranger station. (Pg 26, J2, Q2)

Parking: Park admission is $2.00 for day use. Park in the day use lot.

Swimming area: Salmon Hole is in the West River. Another swimming hole is a short hike upstream in a bend in the West River.

Visitor Guide:
Size & depth of pool: 4
No. & height of waterfalls: 3
Ease of location & access: 4
Uniqueness of features: 5

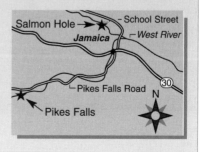

Nicole Laliberte swims below the water's surface in the main pool of Pikes Falls. The rocks are magnified by water.

Pikes Falls

Located on the North Branch Brook, Pikes Falls offers the same type of swimming common in Northern Vermont. A deep pool along with a number of graceful waterfalls have made this a trip worth taking.

The fan-shaped pool, deepest at the base of the waterfall, remains deep enough to swim in even during a dry summer. The eastern side of the pool has a variety of stones for sun worshippers to bathe on.

Visitors can see firsthand how a few rocks can change the direction and flow of a waterway.

Several boulders are placed in the waterfalls during the spring runoff from Stratton Mountain. Unmoved by a normal flow, they stay trapped in the crevices. Several of the falls benefit from the blockage, which causes a backfill that fills the narrow channels causing the water to spill out over the smooth rock. This creates a misty waterfall usually only conducive with heavy-flow streams.

In other places, the water is forced in awkward directions creating bubbling noises. Depending on where you stand, these noises sound different.

The brook flows over a knoll that has been stripped to the bedrock. The smooth rolling surface coincides with the surrounding hillside.

Directions: Take Pikes Falls road 4.6 miles from Route 30 in Jamaica. The trail to the swimming hole is on the same side of the road. (Pg 26, J1, Q3)
Parking: Just after a blind driveway sign on the right, there is a small pull off on the left side of the road to park.
Swimming area: The lower pool is the only place to swim.

Visitor Guide:
Size & depth of pool: 4
No. & height of waterfalls: 4
Ease of location & access: 3
Uniqueness of features: 3

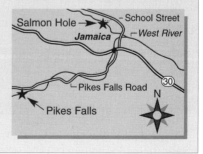

The waterfalls at Stickney Brook will leave travelers straining for comparisons — none of which will ever be found.

Stickney Brook

For country kids, wondering what it would be like to walk on the bottom of a drained river or lake ranks up there with wondering where babies come from.

The Stickney Brook swimming hole most nearly matches that feeling of walking on a dried river bed. Even during the wettest summer, water can't cover the entire flat stepped stream. Where the water most often travels, moss grows and covers these shallow channels in a deep green velvet. Most of the upper falls are small and covered completely with water-filtering moss. The water drips so clear and steady that it appears to be coming from a faucet. Close your eyes at the upper falls, and you will imagine a larger waterfall. The sound of the falls is intensified by the sound reflecting off the bedrock and the impact of the flat landing after a sharp drop.

The shallow flow contributes to the back-and-forth path of water. The main falls is a 12-foot cascading falls that is very airy for about eight feet.

To the west of the waterfall, a huge stone wall accents the layered rock formation of the area. Although not the natural amber color of the delicately banded stream rock, the dark stone appears to have been taken from the woods nearby.

Less than a quarter of a mile downstream from here the brook meets the West River.

Directions: Take Stickney Brook Road in Dummerston .1 of a mile to the first pull off on the right. (Pg 22, F6, Q2)
Parking: Park on the right side of the road. There is room for three vehicles only.
Swimming area: The majority of the pools are less than three-feet deep. If wading makes you happy or if you have children, then this hole is for you.

Visitor Guide:
Size & depth of pool: 1
No. & height of waterfalls: 5
Ease of location & access: 4
Uniqueness of features: 5

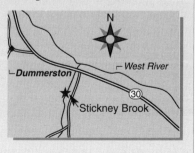

Although swimming is not allowed, visitors at Texas Falls are treated to bowls lit by tall slow-flowing waterfalls.

Texas Falls

(swimming prohibited)

Texas Falls is nature's oasis in the middle of the wild Green Mountain National Forest. This magical place at first seems ruined by the stone trails and bridges that scar its surface. But at second glance one realizes that a place with this much attractive power could be damaged by visitors if it were not for the paths and bridges.

Although swimming is not allowed here, it does not deter people from visiting. The beauty of Texas Falls is in the five waterfalls and bowled bedrock. With drops of seven, six, ten, eight and five feet, the waterfalls are as impressive as ones ten times their size. Each offers something different.

What really makes this place unique are the narrow chutes in the bedrock. At one waterfall, the water slides through a chute and into a pool hidden by the bulbous stone.

From the lowest falls, the entire flume and all the waterfalls rise up the mountain. This is the best spot for photographs.

If you stay here long enough, chances are you will notice the thick moss on the rocks along the gorge. The moss is over 200 years old.

Had the paths not been built to keep visitors off of the rock, the moss no doubt would have been damaged.

Directions: Take Route 125 in Hancock 2.9 miles west. Turn right at the sign for Texas Falls and travel .4 of a mile. The waterfalls are across the road.
(Pg 33, D14, Q1)
Parking: Parking is available on the south side of the road.
Swimming area: Swimming is prohibited.

Visitor Guide:
Size & depth of pool: 4
No. & height of waterfalls: 5
Ease of location & access: 4
Uniqueness of features: 5

The main overlook for Big Falls, top left, gives visitors an impressive view of the falls and lower gorge.

Big Falls

(swimming prohibited)

If you are interested in seeing one of the largest waterfalls in Vermont that isn't covered by a manmade dam, then you may want to visit Big Falls in Troy.

The falls are part of the Missisquoi River and are on a section of the river that flows north. Also known as Troy Falls, Big Falls lets visitors share in the making of Northern Vermont's most powerful river. Upstream from the falls, the Bugbee, Coburn and Beetle Brooks meet to form the Missisquoi. Downstream in small towns along the way, Vermonters have built dams to generate electricity to run their towns.

A trail leads from the parking lot to the main waterfall. Visitors aren't often seen standing on the edge of the gorge looking over. Doing so is always disorienting. Since the waterfall shakes the ground so much that it almost feels like an earthquake, visitors drop to their bellies to look over. If you are a bit squeamish when it comes to heights, steer clear of the chasm wall. There is a trail, which offers a nice view, that leads to the bottom of the falls.

(*Don't bring children.*)

Directions: Take Vielleux Road, just south of the junction to Route 105 on Route 101, in Troy. Go 1.2 miles on Vielleux Road and turn left onto River Road and go another 1.3 miles to a pull off. (Pg 53, B11, Q1)
Parking: Park under the tall pines on the West side of the road.
Swimming area: Swimming is prohibited. The current is extremely dangerous.

Visitor Guide:
Size & depth of pool: 5
No. & height of waterfalls: 5
Ease of location & access: 4
Uniqueness of features: 5

Moss Glen Falls in Granville has become one of the most popular tourist stops during fall foliage.

Moss Glen Falls *(Granville)*

(swimming prohibited)

If you travel from southern to northern Vermont on Route 100, you will pass Moss Glen Falls in Granville and Stowe.

Although it is possible to miss Stowe's version of the falls, you won't miss Granville's, because it is only a few feet from Route 100. Granville has twin falls with the most southern of two waterfalls falling into a shallow pool. This waterfall provides a great backdrop for photographs.

Both falls appear green from the algae that grows on the rocks. If you bring children here, ask them to point out rocks with little moss or algae on them. This can be a great way to get them interested in small life forms. Route 100 runs through a valley near the falls. The water from the falls actually drops sharply over a ledge and into the valley.

The waterfalls are the busiest during fall foliage but are never so crowded in the summer that the atmosphere of the area is destroyed.

The large deck and walkway that visitors stand on below the falls is made out of recycled grocery bags. The material lasts longer than traditional materials because it is resistant to rotting and impervious to corrosion.

Directions: Take Route 100 north from Granville to Moss Glen Falls.
(Pg 34, A1, Q1)
Parking: The parking area is on the west side of road.
Swimming area: Swimming is prohibited.

Visitor Guide:
Size & depth of pool: 1
No. & height of waterfalls: 5
Ease of location & access: 5
Uniqueness of features: 5

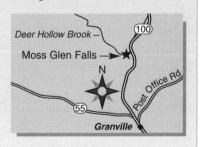

The clear cool pools and narrow chutes of Hamilton Falls make it a terrific day trip for hikers.

Hamilton Falls
(swimming prohibited)

Chances are if you visit Hamilton Falls in the early spring you won't see another person. If you are lucky enough to get this place all to yourself, sit on the stream bank and listen to the waterfalls. They will speak to you — in what way I will leave for you to decide.

A hike from Jamaica State Park is needed to truly appreciate the falls and the feelings of discovery. The three-mile hike leaves hikers in an endorphin high that helps them get in touch with the way things used to be. The rugged terrain surrounding the falls is a reminder of how the land was formed. Every hill at one time or another was shaped by water. The steep banks of Hamilton Falls are still undergoing the process of change that has helped to make the falls one of the most geologically unique areas in Vermont.

The falls are no longer open to swimming due to 14 deaths here. ***Do not walk on the slanted rock around the falls.***

The best view of the falls is beside the lower pool. The constant flow of water through the narrow chutes is hypnotic. The movement of water, like the wind, can be gentle or strong.

When planning a trip, Hamilton Falls should be at the top of everyone's list.

Directions: Take Depot Street .4 of a mile to Jamaica State Park. Ask for a map of the park at the ranger station. You can hike to the falls, or drive to it (see map). (Pg 26, I3, Q3)
Parking: Park in the the day use lot of Jamaica State Park or on West Windham Road.
Swimming area: Swimming is prohibited.

Visitor Guide:
Size & depth of pool: 3
No. & height of waterfalls: 5
Ease of location & access: 3
Uniqueness of features: 5

Index

The author is a native Vermonter, whose love for the outdoors has inspired him to share it with others. He believes that in order for people to take an active interest in protecting the environment they must first have a love for it. In many ways an idealist, he hopes that when the time comes to protect these areas people will stand together. The threat to many swimming areas is real. At the time of this book's printing, Bingham Falls (cover photo) was for sale.

The author decided to do this book while in New York attending Syracuse University. After spending several years away from Vermont, he had an overwhelming desire to return to the state for the project. In the spring of 1997, he purchased a slide-in camper for his truck and went town to town asking about swimming holes.

By summer's end he ran out of money and his primary camera was rendered nearly useless.

He now works at the Burlington Free Press and freelances for *Vermont Life, Runner's World, Chevy Outdoors* and *Draft Horse Journal.* He has a bachelor's degree in journalism from the University of South Florida and a master's degree in photography from Syracuse University.

— Bill Jacko

To order copies of the book, please send your name, address, telephone number and check to:

Jason Minor
RR1 Box 260
Swanton, VT 05488
Fax: 802-868-3782

or check out the web @
swimmingholes.com

Price per book:
$14.95+ tax .75 + $1.00 shipping = $16.70

— For large orders, check out the web for discounts.

Notes